A
Christmas Classic
Celebration

*Candlelight Service
For Christmas Eve*

Roy Caudill

CSS Publishing Company, Inc., Lima, Ohio

A CHRISTMAS CLASSIC CELEBRATION

ISBN 0-7880-1291-6   PRINTED IN U.S.A.

*Dedicated to the
United Church of Canistota,
South Dakota*

Introduction

A *Christmas Classic Celebration* is a unique candlelight service for Christmas Eve. It incorporates scenes of Christmas that are all around us. The service moves from the annunciation to the joy of Jesus' birth. The theme expressed in the service is that Jesus is *in* the world but not *of* the world. As each scene of the service is presented, the worship leader should give a few words of introduction which will help continuity and flow. Meditations can be adjusted to meet local situations or current world events. Popular Christmas songs, such as "Silver Bells," "I'll Be Home For Christmas," "Do You Hear What I Hear?" and "All I Want For Christmas Is My Two Front Teeth" may be sung, using a soloist or song leader singing the verses while the congregation joins in on the refrains. Most of the words to these songs are in people's hearts. If the lyrics are to be printed in a bulletin then permission must be obtained from the following:

"Silver Bells"
    Hal Leonard Corporation
    7777 W. Bluemound Road
    P.O. Box 13819
    Milwaukee, WI 53213
    (414) 774-3630 — Phone
    (414) 774-3259 — Fax
    hlcopyright@halleonard.com — E-mail

"All I Want For Christmas Is My Two Front Teeth" and
"I'll Be Home For Christmas"
    Licensing Department
    Warner Brothers Pub.
    P.O. Box 4340
    Miami, FL 33014

"Do You Hear What I Hear?"
Licensing Department
ARC Music Group
254 West 54th Street
New York, NY 10019

A CHRISTMAS CLASSIC CELEBRATION

Prelude

Welcome and Announcements

THE ANNUNCIATION

Scripture   Luke 1:26-38

Song *(Choir)*   "A Christmas Classic Celebration"*
(Note: If a choir is not available, have the congregation sing "O Come, All Ye Faithful." Sing all verses except the last.)

Evening Prayer *(Unison)*
Most loving God, this evening we celebrate the coming of your Son into the world. We know He is in the world. We are thankful He is not of the world. Oh, how we wish we could be the same. This evening, open our hearts to hear you through the sounds of the world, through the words of scripture, and through the Son whose birth we celebrate this night, and in whose name we pray. Amen.

EXPECTATIONS

Scripture   Isaiah 9:2-6

Meditation 1

Song   "Come, Thou Long-Expected Jesus"

7

CITY SCENES

Song   "Silver Bells"

Meditation 2

Song   "O Little Town Of Bethlehem"

THE WISH

Song   "All I Want For Christmas Is My Two Front Teeth"
(Note: Have all children present stand and sing the
song. Then sing it again with the congregation join-
ing in.)

Meditation 3

Song   "Good Christian Friends, Rejoice"

THE HOPE

Song   "I'll Be Home For Christmas"

Meditation 4

Song *(Choir)*   "Infant Holy, Infant Lowly"
(Note: If a choir is unavailable have the congrega-
tion sing.)

THE HEARING

Song   "Do You Hear What I Hear?"

Meditation 5

Song   "Angels We Have Heard On High"

GOOD NEWS

Scripture   Luke 2:1-7

Prayer Of Confession *(Unison)*
Gracious God, we confess that we have not always loved you with
our whole hearts. Your light has not always shined through us.
Forgive us. As we receive this light, may the light of your Son be
rekindled within us for all the world to see. In Jesus' name we
pray. Amen.

Song   "Silent Night! Holy Night!"
(Note: Light the candles among the congregation as
the hymn is sung. Remain in candlelight through the
sixth meditation. Extinguish the candles as you stand
to sing "Joy To The World.")

> Silent night, holy night!
> All is calm, all is bright
> Round yon virgin mother and child.
> Holy infant, so tender and mild,
> Sleep in heavenly peace,
> Sleep in heavenly peace.
>
> Silent night, holy night!
> Shepherds quake at the sight;
> Glories stream from heaven afar,
> Heavenly hosts sing Alleluia!
> Christ, the Savior, is born!
> Christ, the Savior, is born!
>
> Silent night, holy night!
> Son of God, love's pure light;
> Radiant beams from thy holy face,
> With the dawn of redeeming grace,
> Jesus, Lord, at thy birth,
> Jesus, Lord, at thy birth.

Silent night, holy night!
Wondrous star, lend thy light;
With the angels let us sing,
Alleluia to our King.
Christ, the Savior, is born!
Christ, the Savior, is born!

Scripture John 1:1-5, 10-14

Meditation 6

Song "Joy To The World"

Benediction
Pastor: Christ is in the world
Congregation: We are in the world
Pastor: The world does not know Him
Congregation: They will know him through us.
Pastor: Go! Take him to the world, and may God grant
you a blessed Christmas.
Congregation: And to you a Christ-filled New Year!

Benediction Response Tune: "We Wish You A Merry Christmas"
We wish you a blessed Christmas
We wish you a blessed Christmas
We wish you a blessed Christmas
and a Christ-filled New Year.
God's blessings to you
wherever you are;
God's blessings for Christmas
and a Christ-filled New Year!

Postlude

*Source: "Christmas Classic Celebration," arranged by Patrick M.
Liebergen, Alfred Publishing, Sanctuary Series, 1996.

Meditation 1

Christmas is a time of expectation. Just think of the children's song "Santa Claus Is Coming To Town." It's about expectation. It's about mystery and wonder. This year I wonder. I wonder what expectations the children have. Just recently we read in the local paper some of the children's letters.

One child wrote: I want a baby sister. I want a little train set. I want the world to be free. I want homeless people to have homes. I want warm clothes. Merry Christmas.

Another child wrote: I want some cars, a Nintendo 64, a horse, a lizard, and a good Christmas with lots of presents. I want three snakes, two rats, and 100 sharks. Let there be no fights.

That made me wonder even more. One year, as each Advent candle was lit, a congregation in a local church sang, "Four more weeks till he arrives; three more weeks till he arrives," and so on. I wondered: Who do the children think **HE** is?

I also wondered what God would have us do in the lives of the children. Do we stamp out misplaced wonder, mystery, and expectations? Or, do we help them grow in wonder by helping them hear the words of the prophets, that which we read, and others such as, "The virgin will be with child and will give birth to a son and will call him Immanuel." Can we help the children to discover the wonder and mystery of God? Can we see it for ourselves and join all hearts together in expectation as we sing, "Come, Thou Long-Expected Jesus"?

Meditation 2

A Midwest newspaper ran the following headline: "After a month of bad weather SHOPPING STORM to descend upon the city today." It appeared three days before Christmas. What would shoppers find? Well, the city would be dressed in holiday style; decorations everywhere; snow everywhere; in many ways a feeling of Christmas. But would they find smile after smile and children laughing? I'm not so sure. Regardless of what the shoppers found, it was probably quite a scene.

Two thousand years ago the city was Bethlehem. Joseph and Mary didn't want to be there, but a census was to be taken. They had to go. The city was bustling. The hotels and motels were bursting. On every street corner you heard: "Is there any room in the inn?" The answer came back: "NOOOOOOOO!" Tired and weary, Joseph and Mary found a stable. Clean straw for themselves, some for the manger. The sun went down, the town settled, but Mary did not, for the time had come for the baby to be born, and she gave birth to her firstborn, a son. She wrapped him in cloths and placed him in the manger. Christmas had come to the city.

Meditation 3

"Want" is a word we hear a lot this time of year. Wives ask husbands, husbands ask wives, children ask parents, people ask children: "What do you want for Christmas?" The question may be asked out of curiosity, or it may be asked in hopes of obtaining ideas so that the perfect gift may be bought and presented.

The song we just sang is about a child, a child who has a gap in his teeth. The gap makes it hard to speak properly, and how this child wants to speak. The child wants to speak clearly, wants his words to be understood. The child wants in order to give. The wanting is not selfish; something is wanted so that something can be shared with others. The child wants to wish everyone a Merry Christmas. The child wants everyone to share the joy of the day, and to that end the message must be clear.

The song we are about to sing wants to make the message clear. We are asked to heed the words: "Jesus Christ is born today." We are asked to hear: "He has opened heaven's door/ And you are blessed for evermore./ Jesus Christ was born for this." We are told what we need: "Release from fear of the grave/ Jesus Christ was born to save."

What if we were to put all of that in a child's song that wanted for only one reason: to wish for others? Maybe it would go something like this: *(Sing the song)*

> *All I want for Christmas is my God with me,*
> *My God with me, oh, my God with me.*
> *All I want for Christmas is my God with me*
> *so I could wish all a blessed Christmas.*

Good Christian friends, a child is born; the child speaks. God is with us. It's a good reason to rejoice.

Meditation 4

Dreams! Mistletoe, a place for expressions of love. Snow? Well, it depends on where you live. Some have quite enough already this year, thank you; others dream of snow. But no matter where you are, being home for Christmas is special. Yet, for some it is only a dream. But sometimes dreams come true.

Long ago, Joseph dreamed. Remember how his hopes and dreams had been shattered? The woman he was to marry was pregnant. It wasn't his child. But in a dream, God came to Joseph and said, "Don't be afraid to take Mary home as your wife, for the child she carries is from the Holy Spirit. She will give birth to a son. You are to give him the name Jesus because he will save the people from their sins."

Who would have thought that in a lowly infant child God so holy would reside? In him the love light gleams, and all who draw near will find a home for Christmas. And they will soon discover that it's not a dream.

Meditation 5

The shepherds were in the fields near Bethlehem. They were doing what shepherds do — watching their flocks. Suddenly, one angel of the Lord appeared to them. All it took was one to scare the daylights out of them. "Don't be afraid," the angel said. "I bring you good news of great joy that will be for all people. Today in the town of David a Savior has been born to you. He is Christ the Lord. This will be a sign to you: You will find a baby wrapped in cloths and lying in a manger."

As the shepherds stood in awe the angel was joined by a heavenly host. No angel solo would do. The heavenly host appeared, praising God and singing: "Glory to God in the highest, and on earth peace to those on whom God's favor rests." But look around the world. Where's the peace the angels sang about? Where's the good will?

In Wilmington, Delaware, two teenagers give birth to a son. The baby is born healthy but dies of skull fractures and brain injuries. The body is found in a trash bin. The two are accused of murder.

Over the past few years there have been 280 cases of church arson. One hundred and twelve people, two thirds of them white, have been arrested. Authorities report that racist motivation was clear in about half of the 130 cases of black church arson. Are these attitudes being imparted to children? Is a new generation being raised on hatred?

Recently it was reported that new drugs were tested on Native American children without asking permission or informing people as to what was taking place.

War continues to take lives all over the globe. Adult conflict threatens the lives of the world's children.

A child, a child somewhere shivers in the cold. Realities of life? Bring him silver and gold? Hardly — the world has plenty of that. But take the silver and gold, redeem it, and purchase other gifts for the children: a warm coat, a hot meal, a good education, a safe haven. Give them a hug, love them, and bring them goodness and light.

Why is goodwill and peace so hard to come by? Maybe it's because people don't listen. The angels keep singing, but God's peace and good favor can only rest upon those who hear them sing.

15

Meditation 6

The world is not a perfect place. It was not a perfect place when Jesus was born. But every story surrounding the manger has one message. CHRIST IS BORN! He is in the world. The world did not know him. The world may still not know him, but he is still in the world. Through his death and resurrection Good News was completed. The cradle led to a cross which led to an empty tomb. Darkness gave way to light, and silent night gave way to holy light and life. The Word, Jesus Christ, dwells among us. We have seen his glory, the glory of the One and Only, who came from the Father, full of grace and truth.

JOY TO THE WORLD! THE LORD IS COME!